Five Great Gifts of Whole Life Insurance

Benefits Found *Only* In Whole Life Insurance

That Other Cash Value Life Insurance, Investment, and Financial Products only Dream of Offering

by Jeffrey Reeves, MA
EUREKONOMICS™.com

Five Great Gifts of Whole Life Insurance

by Jeffrey Reeves, MA

For more information, contact Poor Richard Publishing 1270 Jasmine St., Denver CO 80220 — (303)355-0550 Jeffrey.Reeves@USA.net

Published by Poor Richard Publishing Co. Denver, CO Printed in the United States of America 1st Printing

Author: Jeffrey Reeves, MA Cover Design: Sandra Reeves of Poor Richard Publishing.

ISBN-13: 978-0979770937 ISBN-10: 0979770939 Library of Congress Control Number : 2011901043

‘Tis the season…

Illustrating the power, flexibility, and versatility of participating whole life insurance is my 2011 gift to my family,
my clients, my peers, and my country.

I hope this gift keeps on giving through 2011 and for
decades beyond.

December 2010 - *Jeffrey Reeves*

TABLE OF CONTENTS

THE FIRST GIFT

Americans Really Want – MORE MONEY...   1

THE SECOND GIFT

Americans Really Want – FEWER HASSLES...   5

THE THIRD GIFT

Americans Really Want – MORE TIME...   11

THE FOURTH GIFT

Americans Really Want – MORE CHOICES...   15

THE FIFTH GIFT

Americans Really Want – NO WORRIES...   19

A CASE STUDY

EUREKONOMICS™ - The Safe and Easy Path to Prosperity   21

Mortgage Example - The Spreadsheet...   25

AFTERWORD   27

The Template…

I've chosen to use THE FIVE LIFESTYLE ATTRIBUTES THAT REALLY MATTER:

- MORE MONEY
- FEWER HASSLES
- MORE TIME
- MORE CHOICES
- NO WORRIES

from Frank Luntz's eye-opening and best-selling book *What Americans Really Want…Really*[1] as the template for this essay. I chose this format to demonstrate how participating whole life insurance is the only financial product that lets American families create the lifestyle they "Really Want…Really."

---

[1]   ©2009 Frank I. Luntz, pp 47-48, Hyperion Press, NY, NY

The First Gift

Americans Really Want – More Money...

Americans have been led to believe that money can be compartmentalized—mortgage money in home equity, retirement money and college funding in investments, savings in bank CDs, vacation and major purchases on credit cards or who knows where. Americans have lost track of the essential fact that only money is money; access to, use of, and control of their money is essential.

Americans have also been bamboozled into thinking that it makes sense to give control of their money to strangers like Bernie Madoff, some off-the-street rookie from a Behemoth financial corporation with a big advertising budget, or an anonymous money manager at an obscure mutual fund.

BUNK!

Nothing in those strategies reflects the common sense that Benjamin Franklin and the Founders and Builders of America applied to their money issues; common sense reflected in Franklin's *The Way to Wealth*[2]:

> "But with our industry we must likewise be steady, settled, and careful, and oversee our own affairs with our own eye, and not too much to others..."

[2]   https://www.createspace.com/3434860

1

"…and again, Not to oversee workmen, is to leave them your purse open.

Trusting too much to others' care is the ruin of many; for in the affairs of this world men are saved, not by faith, but by the want of it; but a man's own care is profitable; for, If you would have a faithful servant, and one that you like, serve yourself…"

~ Benjamin Franklin in the persona
of Father Abraham

Having a foundation of money that you and you alone control means you can handle the mortgage, retirement, college for the kids, taxes, insurance deductibles, or any of life's surprisingly unsurprising surprises that come your way.

The question then becomes, "Where can Americans put their money so it is readily available—without restrictions or limitations—for all of the uses mentioned above?"

The answer is, *"What Americans really want…really, is participating whole life insurance."*[3]

Unlike most other cash value insurance products or tax qualified savings programs like 401(k)s, IRAs, 529 Plans, etc., participating whole life insurance…

- gives you control of your money

- removes the risk of loss

- eliminates penalties or taxes when you want to use the money that you have saved in your policy

---

[3]   To learn more about participating whole life insurance visit http://bit.ly/Whole-Life

The money you save in a participating whole life insurance policy is your money and you can use it any way you want, any time you want. Moreover, unlike most investments, whole life insurance is worth more at the end of each year than it was at the beginning of the year—*guaranteed!*

Oh, and by the way, your money grows tax free and it's *tax free when you take it out to use it.*[4]

---

[4]   Your EUREKONOMICS™ agent can explain the details.

THE SECOND GIFT

Americans Really Want – FEWER HASSLES...

Accessing your money and controlling your personal economy shouldn't be a hassle for everyday Americans.

- Have you applied for a mortgage recently—say in the past decade—and been faced with demands for information, tax returns, pay stubs, income, assets, and cash flow as well as dozens of forms required by the failed Behemoths in government and lending?

- Have you become obsessive about your *credit reports and scores*—yes you have to worry about more than one—for fear of having your opportunities for employment and credit compromised?

- Has a credit card company arbitrarily raised your rate or cancelled your card because of a *periodic review?*

- Have you tried to buy or lease a car only to discover that you need half a day—minimum—to complete the process and then discovered that, in addition, the interest rate you expected to pay is higher than anticipated by one or two percent...or more?

- Are you—like me and many other Americans—angered by having to pay an ATM machine two dollars so you can get twenty dollars in cash? Does a ten percent fee sound more like a pay day loan than a fair charge?

- Does it make sense for you to have to bow to the seemingly unceasing demands for information and absolute commitments laid upon Americans by Behemoth lenders in order to access *your* equity in *your* home or other real property?

- Is it fair that your money in your retirement account, annuity, or universal life insurance policy should be off limits to you unless you pay penalties, taxes, and or fees?

- Should the money you want to save for your children's education and your own future be at great risk in stocks, commodities, and mutual funds while the Behemoth that sells and gets paid for selling you these risky products—yes, they are products just like a TV or a couch—bears none of the risk?

- Finally—excuse the pun—does it make sense to pay your taxes for a lifetime and then have the same Behemoth government, which took your income for decades, confiscate one-third or more of the money you saved during your lifetime: money that you planned to pay forward when you die to those you care most about?

Using your money and controlling your assets shouldn't be so cumbersome and painful; shouldn't be a hassle; shouldn't—above all—be controlled by Behemoths.

Look carefully at the money related hassles that beset Americans every day. What do you see? *Behemoths!*

Behemoths that either insinuate themselves into your financial life with self-serving schemes and advertising dreams or inject themselves into your personal economy with onerous self-serving laws and worrisome regulations—all the time telling you to "pay no attention to that man behind the curtain."[5]

BUNK!

There are two parties to every financial transaction the Behemoths design and promote…

- The individual American that has earned money and wishes to save it or put it to use
- One or more American Behemoths that want to control both the money and the process that controls the use of the money.

Think about it. Is that what you really want…really?

- You want the savings…right?
- You want the products: the mortgage and the house, the vacation, the car, the fancy wedding, the comfortable retirement, stuff in general…right?
- But…do you want the Behemoths as your partner?
  - » Do you really want to pay interest as high as 29.99%?
  - » Do you really want to complete applications that embarrass you and invade your privacy?

---

[5]   Wizard of Oz, 1939, Warner Bros.

» Do you really want to risk your savings in financial products that guarantee only that they guarantee nothing?

» Do you really want to give up control of the money that flows through your life?

I think not.

***What Americans really want…really is participating whole life insurance.*[6]**

Participating whole life policies are designed in such a way that they allow you to minimize and eventually eliminate all of your credit relationships by using the cash values that you accumulate in your own policies…

- instead of using credit for…
    » purchases made with credit cards

    » auto loans

    » vacations

    » college funding

    » first and second mortgages and equity lines of credit

    » business purchases and expenses

    » emergencies and opportunities
- instead of investing in risky products
- instead of paying taxes
    » on current growth

---

[6]   Ibid – footnote No. 2

> » on retirement income

> » on the money you pay forward to those you care most about

- instead of and any other use of your hard earned money that you can imagine

In other words, using whole life insurance policies is an alternative to the conventional wisdom devised by the Behemoths: conventional wisdom that creates the hassles Americans experience when they give up control of their money.

Using whole life insurance as the foundation for your personal economy empowers you—and every American—to act as your own personal and family *bank* and control the flow of money throughout your lifetime and that of your heirs as well.

The Third Gift

Americans Really Want – More Time…

A discussion that focuses on the issue of *more time* would be incomplete without a reference to Benjamin Franklin's *The Way To Wealth*…

> Father Abraham continues: "If time be of all things the most precious, wasting time must be, as Poor Richard says, the greatest prodigality;"
>
> ~ Benjamin Franklin

How much time do Americans waste doing the bidding of Behemoths?

- filling out forms and waiting in lines at the department of motor vehicles or some other government agency
- completing loan applications
- preparing taxes
- reviewing credit statements
- wrestling with a customer service representative (that is most likely overworked and underpaid)
- verifying purchases and line items on bills and bank statements

- checking credit reports and filing reports to correct errors

- applying for college grants, scholarships, and loans

…need I go on?

The Behemoths tell us that it's all necessary to function in the free enterprise system. However, when you question that necessity, what becomes apparent is that it is necessary *only* for the Behemoths to maintain *their* grasp on *your* money. That's…

BUNK!

Imagine if you will…

- an administrative and financial system that does not require you to waste your time paying attention to many, perhaps most of the demands of the Behemoths…

- a personal economic model that you manage and control

- an approach to money that *guarantees* annual growth without demanding that you personally pay attention

- a reservoir of money that is readily accessible…

   » for whatever reason you choose

   » does not require an application or proof that you qualify

   » allows you to repay what you use on your own schedule

***What Americans really want…really is participating
whole life insurance.*[7]**

Americans that employ a financial model that puts participating whole life insurance at its foundation—we call this
model EUREKONOMICS™—can eliminate many hours of
wasted time and an even greater portion of the frustration
that accompanies the fruitless exercise of slavishly comply-
ing with the incessant demands of the Behemoths for more
of your patience, time, money…more of everything.

More of YOU!

EUREKONOMICS™ frees Americans from the need to
spend their time and energy…

- applying for loans
- paying attention to credit card bills—other than for
  short term cash flow
- concerning themselves with credit scores—al-
  though most who practice EUREKONOMICS™
  maintain exemplary credit without trying
- spending hours and emotion—not to mention
  money—groveling for access to…
    - » home equity
    - » retirement funds in the event of emergen-
      cies or opportunities
- worrying about the tax consequence of every financial decision they make

---

[7]   Ibid – footnote No. 2

- trying to fathom the dark and tangled paths in the caverns of *investment opportunities*—gold, real estate, mutual funds, stocks, hedge funds, indexed insurance and annuity products, and on and on…

You can reduce the time you spend for the benefit of the Behemoths to a minimum. You improve your life in the process; more time, energy, and emotion for your family, exercise, meal preparation, relaxation, reading, writing, visiting, a stop at the coffee shop with a friend…or anything else—*you choose.*

The Fourth Gift

Americans Really Want – More Choices…

21st century Americans encounter more consumer choices in a day than the Founders and Builders of America faced in a year—perhaps a lifetime. By the time I was a child in 1950 beginning the second of my seven decades of life the choices had increased geometrically.

The coffee choices in 1950 were Maxwell House, Folgers, or Chock Full-O-Nuts whether you were at home, grandma's house or the local diner. In 1750 coffee was rare and had no brand name. Today the list of coffees Americans can choose would fill several pages of this essay.

The same holds true for almost every product and service available in America…

- Autos—a couple of dozen options in 1950…hundreds today

- Appliances—99% of the appliances available today were not even invented and patented in 1950

- Electronics—in 1950 there were no computers, no cell phones; only reel to reel tape recorders; portable radios that weighed 20 pounds; a handful of TVs—9" circular screens at that

- Clothing brands were limited to Converse, Levi, Lee, and Wrangler—everything else in the wardrobe was generic;

- In 1950 there was nothing in space but stars and planets and imagined Martian invaders

- This list could also go on for pages

Frank Luntz points out in his book that it's not just choices but—more importantly—*the right to choose* that is ingrained in the American psyche. However, having many options is not always best. "Too many choices" says Frank Luntz "is no choice at all."[8]

This is especially true when it comes to making decisions about how to handle your money. In the first segment of this essay I wrote:

> "Americans have been led to believe that money can be compartmentalized—mortgage money in home equity, retirement money and college funding in investments, savings in bank CDs, vacation and major purchase money on credit cards or who knows where. Americans have lost track of the essential fact that money is money; access to, use of, and control of their money is essential.
>
> Americans have also been bamboozled into thinking that it makes sense to give control of their money to strangers like Bernie Madoff, some off-the-street rookie from a Behemoth financial corporation with a big advertising budget, or an anonymous money manager at an obscure mutual fund."

---

[8] ©2009 Frank I. Luntz, pp 47-48, Hyperion Press, NY, NY

It is this artificial mindset created by the Behemoths *for* the Behemoths that has led 21st century America and many of its citizens to the brink of financial failure. Foreign governments control America's financial future and the American Behemoths want to control the money and finances of American citizens. That creates the environment where "Too many choices is no choice at all."

If Americans want to prosper and actually improve and increase their financial choices, Americans must escape the dungeon of debt and deceit that binds them to Behemoths. That means Americans must change their mind about money and reduce the range of their financial choices in a way that allows them to maintain control of their money and the choices they make about how to employ that money to their advantage and that of their families.

What Americans really want…really is participating whole life insurance.[9]

There are over 15,000 mutual funds, even more individual stocks and bonds, hundreds of indexed funds, thousands of variable, indexed, and current assumption annuities and universal life insurance products, dozens of ways to buy gold and other precious metals, tens of thousands of short term savings products…what's your choice?

Most of the time, your choice is guided by advice from a sales rep. The advice is usually controlled and motivated by a Behemoth. It's a fact; impartial financial advice is rare. Moreover, most Americans—including most who claim the title of *advisor*—do not have the information or education they need to make sound decision from among the

---

[9]   Ibid – footnote No. 2

tens of thousands of financial products that are available in the marketplace.

What all of this points to is that choosing *products*—even though there are many choices—is never going to create abundance and security for 21st century Americans…"it is no choice at all."

The economic principles and financial practices needed for financial success are centuries old. They are found in the *New Testament*, the *Torah*, thousands of secular works like Benjamin Franklin's *The Way to Wealth*, and in the lives of the Founders and Builders of America—the greatest country and economy in the history of the human race.

EUREKONOMICS™ embodies these economic principles and financial practices.

EUREKONOMICS™ gives 21st century Americans a way to build their wealth without risking their future by putting participating whole life insurance as the foundation of their personal economy and financial plan. This still lets American families choose to add any financial product to their portfolio that they feel serves their goals. However, EUREKONOMICS™ does so without risking the money in their foundation on hypothetical investments or insurance products.

THE FIFTH GIFT

Americans Really Want – NO WORRIES…

I doubt there is a single tax-qualified retirement account—a 401(k) for example—mutual fund, or stock portfolio that hasn't experienced a significant loss of value during its life and most assuredly over the past decade.

I also doubt that Americans are comforted by re-assurance from a Behemoth's financial planner or advisor that all will be well "in the long term." Let's face it, the stock market and every product that is driven by the *investment* community are slot machines in Wall Street's and Washington's casinos…and the house always wins.

What Americans really want…really is participating whole life insurance.[10]

Fortunately the Dolts in DC and the Wonks on Wall Street have had to recognize that mutual insurance companies—*that means they are owned by and derive their capital from the policy owners and not outside shareholders*—are among the most stable financial institutions in America and have been so for over 150 years.

Unfortunately, the stockholder owned investment and insurance Behemoths—think Lehman Brothers and AIG—participate in the Wall Street lottery and do not have and

[10]   Ibid – footnote No. 2

cannot produce competitive participating whole life insurance contracts.

So, what do the Behemoths do instead? They flood the market with *products* that they say perform just as well—with the footnote that, unlike participating whole life insurance, they guarantee only that the Behemoths will get paid and that you are guaranteed nothing.

After five decades as a proponent of participating whole life insurance—first as an owner then as an advisor for nearly 40 years—I am confident that there is no other financial product that has the power, flexibility, and versatility to assure its owners *wealth without worry.*

A Case Study

EUREKONOMICS™ - The Safe and Easy Path to Prosperity

Consider This...

Most Americans start their adult lives in rental homes, apartments, or condos. Most don't want to rent and would choose to buy a home but often feel they can't afford to buy—especially in today's economy. Many Americans also lease/rent their automobiles for the same reason.

Term life insurance is like that too. Most Americans rent life insurance—which, like any rented item, makes someone else wealthy and you less wealthy—when they are starting their adult lives because they are led to believe that using term insurance is the best way to acquire *life insurance.*

However, there is a way to *reverse this entire process of renting homes, cars, insurance, and everything else.* You can accelerate your ownership of the items you buy and still use term insurance to protect your spouse and family.

John and Mary—An Example…

John—age 27 and Mary—age 26 were a young couple just like millions of other young couples.[11]   John and Mary owned term life policies to provide extra tax-free money for each other in the unlikely event of a death.

However, John and Mary had also saved $20,000.00 in participating whole life policies for the down payment on a home. They purchased their first home for $200,000.00 and—because the house they purchased was appraised at $250,000.00—they were able to finance 100% of the purchase price.

Since John and Mary didn't need the down payment money for the purchase, they went shopping for their decorating, landscaping and some additional furnishings. They carefully completed all three projects at a cost of just under $12,000.00. They borrowed the $12,000.00 to pay these expenses from their whole life policies.[12]

John and Mary then chose to repay their whole life policy loans at the rate of $300.00 per month including interest. They repaid the loan in less than four years and recovered all of the money they had spent. They also avoided paying hundreds of dollars in interest that would have gone into the pocket of a commercial lender.

---

[11]   John and Mary are fictional characters based on a real couple. The names have been changed to protect identities.

[12]   Policy loans are actually loans from the insurance company against the cash value accumulations in a participating whole life policy. The values of the policy do not decline and the borrowed funds do not eliminate dividends or reduce the guaranteed annual growth within the policy unless the owner surrenders the policy or the insured dies. In those cases, the amount of the loan is deducted from the net proceeds of the policy before they are paid out.

The Story Continues…

That's not the end of the story. In addition to repaying the loan they had taken from their policies they continued to add money to their policies at the rate of $700.00 per month. Just four and one half years later their policies had a loan free balance of over $50,000.00.

Based on their $1,200.00 per month payment during this same period of time, the loan balance on John's and Mary's home had only reduced to $185,000.00. John and Mary decided to use the $50,000.00 from their policy to reduce the mortgage loan. They also decided to refinance the remaining $135,000.00. That reduced their mortgage payment to just over $800.00 per month.

John and Mary continued to put $700.00 into their policy each month. They found their incomes increasing so they also began paying back the $50,000.00 loan from their policy at the rate of $800.00 per month also. In just about 6 years the entire $50,000.00 they had borrowed from themselves was recovered in their policies and the policies had a balance of over $120,000.00 – *enough to pay off the entire mortgage and hold a clear title to their home in fewer than 11 years.*

John and Mary borrowed against their policy values and created a **debt-to-themselves** of $120,000.00. They decided to pay themselves back at the rate of $2,000.00 each month. Just over 5 years later they had recovered all of the money they borrowed from their policies including the interest that they would otherwise have paid to a mortgage company. They also continued to add $700.00 to their policies each month during this time.

The Bottom Line…

John and Mary paid off a $200,000.00 mortgage and put over $200,000.00 into their policies in just 16 years. Between the money in the policy and the equity in their home[13] , John and Mary created an estate value of over $600,000.00 in those 16 years.

If John and Mary continue to contribute to their policies at the same rate and continued to live in the same home until they are at retirement age—another 24 years—*and do nothing else to improve their financial situation*, they'll have about $1,300,000.00 cash in their policies and over $1,000,000.00 in unencumbered home equity[14] . John and Mary, with the guidance of a EUREKONOMICS™ advisor, could create an *after tax* annual income of *over $100,000.00* by combining the income producing ability of both their life insurance and their home equity.

John and Mary will also have other sources of retirement income[15] —Social Security, other savings, some small investments (no mutual funds), and likely inheritances from both sets of parents—that substantially improve their retirement income, assure them of ready cash for emergencies and opportunities, and allow them to create a significant legacy to pay forward to those they care about.

That, my friends, Is EUREKONOMICS™!

---

[13]   This assumes a 4% annual rate of appreciation on their home yielding a value over $400,000.00 in 16 years.

[14]   This also assumes a 4% rate of appreciation on their home.

[15]   Both John and Mary chose to opt out of the tax qualified retirement plans at work because they recognized that many 401(k)s had turned into 201(k)s and they were unwilling to risk their futures in the speculative choices offered by their employers' plans.

Mortgage Example - The Spreadsheet…

The transactions described above with words and numbers may be hard to visualize, so there's a spreadsheet below that illustrates those transactions. The spreadsheet reflects the amounts paid or contributed during the given year and the balances owed or accumulated at the end of each year.

Mortgage Example

End of Year	Mortgage Payments	Mortgage Balance	Net Policy Deposits	Policy Loan Balance	Policy Repay-ments	Policy Cash Balance
1	14,400	197,544	24200	10,200	1,800	9,505
2	14,400	194,937	8400	6,600	3,600	20,567
3	14,400	192.168	8400	3,600	3,600	29,082
4	14,400	189,229	8400	0	3,600	41,250
5	14,400	186,106	8400	0	0	52,874
6	60,706	133.332	8400	41,506	9,600	20,337
7	9,600	131,582	8400	31,906	9,600	39,100
8	9,600	129,713	8400	21,306	9,600	59,070
9	9,600	127,729	8400	11,706	9,600	78,750
10	9,600	125,823	8400	1,106	9,600	100,655
11	9,600	123,387	8400	0	9,600	124,399
12	123,387	0	8400	99,385	24,000	24,266
13	0	0	8400	75,385	24,000	72,660
14	0	0	8400	51,385	24,000	104,684
15	0	0	8400	27,385	24,000	143,920
16	0	0	8400	3,385	24,000	183,933
17	0	0	8400	0	0	204,050

Notes on the chart...

- Calculations were developed in late February 2007 are based on information from BankRate.com and from a major Fortune 500 mutual life insurance company. John's and Mary's actual policies, mortgage, etc. were purchased prior to 2007. The projected numbers are updated here to reflect current market conditions.

- The first year net deposits reflect the $20,000 accumulated plus the $8,400 deposited during the year, minus net borrowed money.

- The actual repayment amounts in years 4 and 11 would be mostly for interest. The interest due is less than amount shown as being paid in those years.

- The repayment amounts in years 12 thru 16 would be less than the total amount due because of the overpayments shown in years 4 and 11.

- Years 6 and 12 reflect a loan at the beginning of the year used to pay down or pay off the mortgage and a payment through the year reducing the policy loan balance.

- The policy balance in year 17 accurately reflects these variances.

Afterword

21st Century Americans face the greatest challenge to their personal wealth and the future of our country since the Civil War.

Just like the Americans of 1865, our challenge is living up to the principles and ideals paid forward to America by its Founders and Builders—principles and ideals that made it the greatest country in the history of the world.

At the same time, we have to face the reality that Behemoths, the very governments and businesses that Americans have relied on to help them stay true to those principles and ideals, have placed their ideologies and self interest ahead of those principles and ideals and have taken over so much of our lives and become so intrusive that they impede our success.

The financial aspect of this challenge is apparent to everyday Americans and their families. The solutions are not.

It's not that the solutions are complex, hard to understand, or difficult to achieve. The challenge for everyday Americans is that the Behemoths of America—government, unions, banks, investment firms, mutual funds, stock insurance companies, lobbyists like AARP, and on and on—these Behemoths have created the myth that they know how to take care of American family finances better than individual American families.

BUNK!

If that were the case, would America be in the financial mess it's in today...

- Would the debt we Americans are paying forward to our children be growing at a trillion dollars— that's one thousand times one billion—per year; almost *three billion dollars a day?*

- Would we allow that debt to be in the hands of foreign governments—some of which are America's sworn enemies?

- Would unemployment be at a steady nine and one half percent or higher for almost two years—with no end in sight?

- Would basic legal rights—property rights, bond-holder rights, "life, liberty, and the pursuit [not guarantee] of happiness"—be at risk?

- Would bankruptcies and foreclosures be soaring?

- Would our current and future health care be so severely at risk

- Would the growth in the number and income of government workers be twice that of everyday Americans seeking and doing the same jobs for capitalized businesses?

- Would individual retirement accounts be bouncing from record highs to record lows and be devoid of any significant guarantees—except, of course, the guarantee that they guarantee commissions and fees to the Behemoths and nothing at all to you?

- Would 2011's tax rates still have been an unknown factor for Americans looking forward with less than ten days left in the 2010 legislative session?

- Would Americans accept the ineptitude in government—especially union controlled government—to rule their lives?

I think not. How about you?

Individual Americans may not be able to turn the Titanic of the Behemoths around but each of us can opt for the lifeboat of EUREKONOMICS™, and minimize the damage to our personal economies.

Learn more at **EUREKONOMICS.com**

EUREKONOMICS™ Books

EUREKONOMICS™ —a term coined by Jeffrey Reeves, combines the power of two ancient Greek words into a unique 21st century term.

- Eureka—means "I found it!"
- Oikonomia—economy in English—means "household management."

Amazingly—and unfortunately—the original meaning of economy has been lost. A volcanic eruption of misinformation and disinformation over the past half century buried the idea that Americans are responsible for their own personal economies.

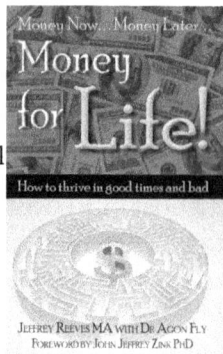

Order your copy of *Money for Life... How to thrive in good times and bad* - a complete education in the Money for Life principles and practices. The book...

- Introduces the villians that survive and thrive by consuming your money for their own benefit.
- Discusses the myths, misrepresentations, and misconceptions of the current failed financial model.
- Defines and describes "personal economy" and shows why every American needs one.
- Studies the financial models that ruled America's economy from the founding of the country and evolved into the failed model that America adopted in the late 20th century.
- Looks at the underpinnings of the Debt Paradigm and insight into how to escape it.
- Discusses how you can free yourself from the dungeon of the Debt Paradigm and introduces cash value life insurance as the preferred "*bank*ing" vehicle in the Money for Life financial model.
- Describes the Four Pillars that support EVERY successful personal economy. Contains extensive and detailed examples drawn from clients and experience of over 30 years.
- Demonstrates how you can deconstruct and reconstruct your personal economy and free up money. Contains several examples, from real life situations, of individuals and families moving from dependence to independence.

The Way to Wealth by Benjamin Franklin

with Commentary by Dr Agon Fly

In 1758, Benjamin Franklin published the 25th and final issue of Poor Richard's Almanac. As a preface to this final edition, he wrote *The Way to Wealth* and introduced Father Abraham as the main character in the tale. Father Abraham embodied the financial wisdom that "Poor" Richard Saunders —one of Benjamin Franklin's many pen names —incorporated in the 25 years during which the almanac was a staple on mantels above fireplaces, in personal libraries and on the tables of colonial America.

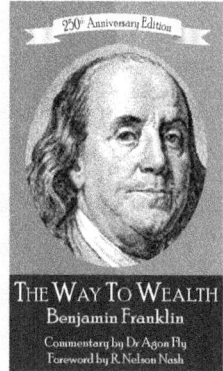

In 2008, on the 250th anniversary year of that event, Dr Agon Fly is adding a unique and timely perspective to this classic book about money and life. The wisdom that Dr. Benjamin Franklin captured in *The Way to Wealth* is timeless. However, the vernacular of 1758 sometimes obscures the meaning for today's economy and for the personal economies of 21st Century Americans. Dr Agon Fly's commentary adds clarity to the language and insights found in The Way to Wealth's tested and true principles and practices. A Commentary on Benjamin Franklin's classic *The Way to Wealth*.

R. Nelson Nash praises this work in his Foreword to The *Way to Wealth,* where he states that the "commentary ranks right alongside George Clason's *The Richest Man in Babylon* as the complete answer to the problems created by the arrogance of the financial community during our times…"

Order both at www.EUREKONOMICS.com

Every American that wonders about their financial future should own a copy of...

The Five Great Gifts of Whole Life Insurance.

"Why?" you ask.

During the past forty years, the Behemoths of Wall Street and Washington tried to bury the knowledge, understanding, and wisdom of whole life insurance under an onslaught of disinformation and misinformation from their cohorts on Madison Avenue.

Their aim?

To gain control of money that rightly belongs to Americans, to their families, and to small businesses.

The Behemoths succeeded in taking millions of Americans down a path that leads to financial servitude. However, they failed to damage the companies and insurance professionals that know what Americans really want, understand how whole life insurance really works...really, and why it belongs at the foundation or every personal economy.

The power, flexibility, and versatility of participating whole life insurance has served and saved the personal economies American families for over one hundred-fifty years. Whether you are a single person, member of a family, matriarch, patriarch, owner of a business, executive at a large company, or an insurance and financial advisor— providing those you care about with their personal copy of *The Five Great Gifts of Whole Life Insurance* is a service they will remember—and appreciate—for a long time.

You may also like to customize...

The EUREKONOMICS™ *Dazzling Dozen*

EUREKa! ecONOMICS - EUREKONOMICS™

The power, flexibility, and versatility of participating whole life insurance has served and saved the personal economies American families for over one hundred-fifty years.

Whether you are a single person, member of a family, matriarch, patriarch, owner of a business, executive at a large company, or an insurance and financial advisor— you will benefit from knowing more about whole life insurance, which has been called 'The Swiss Army Knife of Financial Products" in The Wall Street Journal.

Moreover, you will become a hero by providing those you care about with their personal copy of The Dazzling Dozen. They will remember—and appreciate—your thoughtfulness for a long time.

Contact us at **admin@EUREKONOMICS.com**.

Or call 888-300-9661 for more information.

We will show you how you can economically create a *customized* version of the unique book to pay forward its wealth of wisdom.

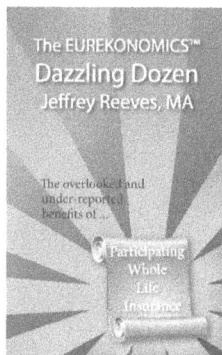

www.ingramcontent.com/pod-product-compliance
Lightning Source LLC
Chambersburg PA
CBHW071435200326
41520CB00014B/3704